Amazon Echo Dot 2nd

Generation Easy Guide

Table of Contents

Introduction

Amazon Echo Dot 2nd Generation is a breakthrough device that can make your life a whole lot easier. If you haven't bought this amazing device yet, then you are certainly missing out on something! It might surprise you, but there are plenty of things that you can do with Amazon Echo Dot.

A flagship device produced by Amazon, it is the second installment of its renowned Echo series. The Echo Dot is a voice-modulated and hands-free device that runs on Alexa (an Artificial Intelligent enabled assistant). From reading the news to setting alarms and accessing information to playing music, there are plenty of things that the Echo Dot device can be used for.

If you have also bought this revolutionary AI-enabled device from Amazon, then your life is about to get extremely convenient. Though, in order to make the most out of Echo Dot 2nd Generation, you should be well-prepared. We are here to help you do the same!

Go through this quick and comprehensive user guide to Amazon Echo Dot 2nd Generation and be an expert in no time. We have given an in-depth walkthrough of almost everything that you can do with this powerful device.

Additionally, to make things easier for you, we have provided various illustrations and pictures in this guide. In a matter of a few minutes, you would be able to learn how to operate your newly bought Echo Dot device. Let's get it started!

Chapter 1 – Getting Started

The second generation of Echo Dot is not just a smarter, but a relatively reasonable Alexa-enabled speaker device. Alexa is known as the highly sophisticated artificial intelligence developed by Amazon. One can say that it is the Amazon's answer to Apple's Siri and Window's Cortana.

The device is specifically designed to serve our everyday needs and is based on a highly-advanced machine learning algorithm. It can be connected to a speaker or headphone via Bluetooth or 3.5 mm jack. It can be connected to Pandora, Spotify, Amazon Music, TunIn, etc. to play music with a simple command.

Also, the device can be used to perform your everyday tasks. You can easily control household gadgets, lights, sprinklers, smart televisions, and more with it. The new Echo Dot also has the ability to recognize your voice from a distance and even in a noisy atmosphere. From being your assistant in the kitchen to letting you know about the traffic updates, this device can do it all.

All you got to do is use your voice to control it. Since it is controlled by Alexa (the AI), you need to give an instruction using the word "Alexa". In simpler terms, "Alexa" is also the trigger (wake command) for the device. Suppose you need to find a Chinese restaurant nearby, then all you got to say is "Alexa, find a Chinese restaurant nearby", "Alexa, find me a Chinese restaurant", or any other command having the same meaning.

Yes! It is really as simple as it sounds. Before we make you understand the integrities related to it, let's first understand the hardware and software specification of the device. In order to know how it works, it is of utmost importance that you know what the device is made up of.

With a weight of just 5.7 oz. it has a compact 3.3" front and a 1.3" base. It has a dual WiFi connectivity and can also be connected to other devices via Bluetooth.

It also has an inbuilt speaker that can be connected to other audio speakers with a 3.5 mm jack. You can further control the device with an Alexa app (available for Android, Fire, and iOS devices).

Just charge it using its power adapter or a USB cable (both come in the box). Its front has four basic buttons – volume up, volume down, microphone on/off, and an action button. The front also has a light ring which gets enabled when the device is in action. The back of the device has a micro USB portal and a 3.5 mm audio output jack.

Alexa is the brain behind the Echo Dot series and gets smarter with every passing day. You can further customize it with its dedicated app. The second generation of Amazon Echo Dot boasts a significant improvement to Echo Dot 1st generation. Not only the device has got cheaper, but it has added various applications as well.

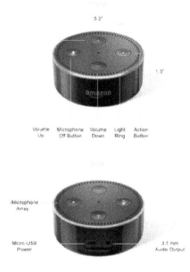

With a smarter OS, it has got a whole new hardware as well. The second generation of Echo Dot features a sleek finish and is enabled by a smarter Alexa. Now when you are well aware of the hardware and software specifications of your newly bought device, let's get you started. Move ahead and learn how to set up your device easily.

Chapter 2 – Setting Up Amazon Echo Dot

The first step is to set up your Amazon Echo Dot device in order to use it seamlessly. Start by placing your device at a respective location. You can place it almost anywhere you want. Ideally, your kitchen counter or a bedroom nightstand would make a perfect place to keep your Echo Dot device.

Set up your device

Though you can use Echo Dot as a standalone device or without other Alexa devices as well, but it won't be able to serve its major function. After unpacking the device and placing it at the desired location, start by configuring it. Turn on your device in order to connect it to your Amazon account. Simply follow these easy instructions to do so.

1. Firstly, you need to download the Alexa app on your device or tablet. The Alexa app is available for free and has been made by Amazon to make it easier for users to control their Echo Dot without any trouble. By using the app you can manage music, set alarms or timers, update shopping lists, and perform a wide range of other tasks. The app is available for Fire OS, Android, and iOS devices. Simply go to the App Store and search for "Alexa app".

2. If you want to access the app from your desktop or any other device, then you can simply visit its official website: https://alexa.amazon.com. You can visit the website from any web browser and can get an access to it from your desktop or laptop. Though, there are a few devices like Kindle Fire (first and second gen), Kindle Fire HD 7" and 8.9" (second gen) that does not support the Alexa app as of now.

3. Now, after successfully installing the app on your tablet or phone, turn on the Echo Dot device. Ideally, you should place your Echo Dot device at least 8-inches away from any wall or window. This makes it easier for the device to recognize your voice. Plug in your Echo Dot device to a secure power outlet using an authentic adapter. This would make the light ring of the device turn blue. After charging it sufficiently, the light ring will turn orange and Alexa will greet you.

4. After charging your device, you need to connect it to a WiFi network. Using your Alexa app, you can connect the device to a desirable WiFi network. There are clear instructions provided in the app that will let you connect the device to a Wifi network. Nevertheless, we have provided an in-depth walkthrough for you to connect Echo Dot to your WiFi network later in our guide.

5. In case your device is not able to recognize the WiFi network, press the Action button and hold it for another 5-7 second. Subsequently, open the Alexa app on your phone. Go to "Settings" and tap on the "Set up a new device" option.

6. If after performing the above-stated steps your Echo Dot device doesn't connect, then try to restart it. You can unplug and plug the device again to make it restart. If the trouble becomes persistent and you are not able to connect your device to the WiFi network, then try to restore it to its Factory Settings. We have provided an easy tutorial to Reset Your Echo Dot later as well.

7. After connecting to your WiFi network, Alexa would be able to receive your commands. Since its wake word is "Alexa", you simply need to say it with a subsequent command. You can alter the wake word to something else (by default it is "Alexa"). To do so, go to the "Settings" options in your app and select "Echo device" option. There, you can select the "wake word" for your device.

8. To get the best results, you can also connect your Echo Dot device to an external speaker. You can do it by either connecting it to a speaker with a 3.5 mm jack or with another Bluetooth speaker wirelessly.

That's it! After performing these easy steps, you would be able to set up your Echo Dot device.

1. Plug in Echo Dot   2. Connect to the internet with the Alexa App   3. Just ask for music, weather, news, and more

Reset your device

If you are not able to set up your Echo Dot device or are facing any problem to connect it, then you might need to reset it. Though Echo Dot 2nd generation is a sophisticated device, but chances are that it might turn unresponsive at times. In order to resolve this issue, you might need to simply reset it. Do this by following these simple instructions:

1. If the device has become unresponsive while getting charged, then simply unplug the power adapter from the device and plug it again after a while.

2. If the above solution won't work, then try to reset it manually. Start by pressing the volume-down and the Microphone button simultaneously. After some 10-20 seconds, the light would turn orange to blue.

3. Wait for a while as the light ring would change its color again and become orange. If the light ring has turned back to orange, then it means that your device has entered the setup mode.

4. Now, you need to connect your device to a WiFi network using the Alexa app.

This would just reset your device and make it responsive again. After resetting it, you would need to follow the same drill by connecting it to a Wifi network. If you are confused about it, then move to the next chapter and learn how to connect your Echo Dot device to a WiFi network.

Chapter 3 – Connecting Your Device

Your Echo Dot can be connected to various other devices as well. Start by connecting it to a WiFi network. If needed, you can connect it to your phone or a Bluetooth speaker. In this section, we will make you learn how to connect your Echo Dot to different networks and devices.

Connecting to a Wifi Network

As stated, in order to set up your Echo device, you need to connect it to a WiFi network. This is how Alexa extracts any information and controls other connected devices. In order to access your commands, process anything, or even stream any media, Alexa needs to be connected to the internet.

Before you connect your device to WiFi, make sure that it is connected to a power outlet. Also, you should already have the Alexa app downloaded on your phone or tablet. The second generation Echo Dot uses the 802.11 a/b/g/n standard to connect to any network and can be connected to dual WiFi 2.4 GHz and 5 GHz networks. Currently, it does not support peer-to-peer (ad-hoc) network connectivity.

In order to connect your device to a WiFi network, just follow these steps:

1. Start by opening the Alexa app on your tablet or phone. Go the "Settings" option, which is located on the left panel.

2. From there, you can select your Echo Dot device. Go to the "Update WiFi" section. Here, you would be given different options. If you are using your WiFi for the first time, you need to set up a new device. To do this, tap on the "Set up a new device" option.

3. Now, you need to make your Echo device ready to get connected. Do this by pressing the "Action" button for 5 seconds. The light ring color would change to orange. This would let you know that your device is now connected to your app. Also, the app would list out all the nearby WiFi networks that your Echo device can get connected to.

4. Tap on the "Connect" option and provide the respective password of your network. After authorization, your Echo Dot would be connected to your network.

5. Sometimes, a device is not able to locate a network or a network is simply hidden. In this case, you need to manually set up a network. If you are not able to see your WiFi name in the list of all the networks, it means you need to manually select it. You can tap on the "Rescan" option at first. If it doesn't work, then scroll down to the "Add a Network" option and provide your WiFi's name and other essential details in order to connect it.

After following these steps, you would be able to connect your Echo Dot device to a WiFi network. Alexa would be activated and would be ready to respond to your commands.

Connecting to an External Speaker

It might surprise you, but you can also use Alexa with another external speaker. This is mostly used when you are playing something from Alexa to another speaker (the vice versa is not possible as of now). You can make it happen by using an audio cable and after following these easy instructions:

1. Make sure that your Echo Dot device and external speakers are placed at least 3-feet away from each other. This is to make sure that Alexa is able to hear the wake word and respond to your command without mixing it with the noise.

2. Now, turn on your external speaker and take an audio cable.

3. Place one end of the cable into the speaker's input and other end to the audio jack of the Echo Dot.

This would make the audio start streaming on the external speaker. Echo Dot has a 3.5 mm audio jack. If your external speaker uses some other jack, then you can use an intermediate adapter to make it work.

Connecting to a Bluetooth Speaker

If connecting your Echo Dot device to another speaker using a cable seems cumbersome to you, then don't worry. You can also connect it to a Bluetooth speaker easily. Before you learn how to do it, make sure that you have placed your Bluetooth speaker at least 3-feet away from your Echo Dot device.

Additionally, Echo Dot can be connected to only one Bluetooth device at a time. If you have already connected it to any other device, then make sure you disconnect it before turning on the Bluetooth speaker. After making sure that you are ready, just follow these steps and connect your Echo Dot to a Bluetooth speaker.

1. Start by turning on the pairing mode on your Bluetooth speaker. Most of the times, it is the default mode.

2. Open the Alexa app on your phone or tablet and go to the "Settings" option.

3. Select the Echo Dot device that you are using presently. Now, go to the "Bluetooth" option and tap on the "Pair a new device" option. This would make your Echo Dot device to enter the pairing mode as well. It will start discovering all the nearby Bluetooth devices with which it can pair.

4. After a while, a list of all the available devices would appear. Out of the provided list, select your Bluetooth speaker. As soon as the Echo Dot device is able to connect to a Bluetooth speaker, Alexa would inform you.

5. Just tap on the "Continue" option in your Alexa app after pairing the devices together. Now, you can just stream media on your Echo Dot and play it on the paired Bluetooth speaker.

6. To disconnect the speaker from the device, simply use the voice command "Disconnect" or do it from the app. Also, you can just connect to the speaker again with a simple "Connect" voice command.

Additionally, you can go to the respective device listed under the "Bluetooth" option in order to manage it. You can add or delete any device easily by doing so.

Connecting to a Mobile Phone

Just like connecting to a Bluetooth speaker, you can also connect your Echo Dot to another mobile device. Though, in this case, you can use your mobile device as a source. For example, if you don't want to stream music online, you can simply connect your mobile device to Echo Dot and use it a source to play your media files.

Before you commence, make sure that your mobile device is compatible with Echo Dot. There is a certified list of devices and standards that the Echo Dot second generation supports, which is provided on its official webpage.

Since Echo Dot can be connected to only one Bluetooth device at a time, make sure that it is disconnected from any other device before you commence. Alexa can be used to stream media from your phone to Echo Dot. Currently, the device doesn't have the access to read your texts, receive calls, or reply to a notification.

Turn on the Bluetooth pairing mode on your mobile phone and simply follow these steps to connect your Echo Dot with your mobile.

1. Start by opening the Alexa app on your device and visit the "Settings" option.

2. Select your Echo Dot device and tap on the "Bluetooth" option. Now, select the "Pair a New Device" to let your Echo Dot enter the pairing mode.

3. Now, go to the home screen of your mobile device. Visit the "Bluetooth" option under Settings. Turn on the Bluetooth and let it search the nearby

devices. It would give a list of all the nearby Bluetooth devices that can be connected. Your Echo Dot device would be one of them. Simply tap on it in order to connect it to your mobile device.

4. After a while, both the devices would be connected. You can further disconnect it, by either turning off the Bluetooth feature of the device or simply telling Alexa to "disconnect".

That' it! After connecting your mobile device to Echo Dot, you can easily stream music to your Echo Dot from your phone.

We are sure that by now you would be able to connect your Echo Dot to different devices. From simply connecting it to your WiFi network to pairing it with other Bluetooth devices – you can now do it all. Move ahead and learn how to make the most out of Alexa in the next chapter.

Chapter 4 – Making Your Life Easier

Now when you are well aware of Echo Dot's basic specifications and can easily configure it or connect it to any other device, let's explore its major features that can make your life a whole lot easier.

There are almost thousands of things that you can do with Alexa. From listening to your favorite songs to turning off the lights, you can do it all. Let's learn it one step at a time. To make things easier, we have assumed that the wake word you have chosen for your device is "Alexa".

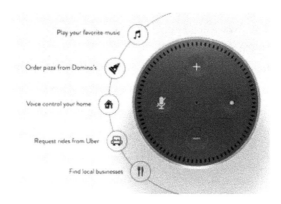

Playing music

When it comes to music, the sky is the limit with Echo Dot. Not only can you stream music, but can update your playlist as well. You can request music from various apps (TuneIn, Spotify, etc.) or can simply play it from your mobile phone. You can either request a particular genre of music, a respective song, music from a particular artist, and so on. Not just that, you can ask Alexa to play music to go along with your mood or a holiday.

Ideally, the device is always listening to you. Since it uses the uniform voice modulation technique, you don't need to shout even if you are standing far from it. Just say the words and Alexa would make it happen. For instance, you can try the following commands:

- Alexa, play songs by Sia

- Alexa, play some Rock music

- Alexa, play dance mix

- Alexa, play my Christmas playlist

You can also give the name of a particular app while playing music. For instance, the following command will play the version of the song from Spotify.

- Alexa, play songs by Celine Dion from Spotify

Needless to say, you can always use commands like "Stop", "Turn the volume up/ down", "Pause", etc. while playing music on Echo Dot.

Creating a smart home

The second generation of Echo Dot can be used to control your household objects. It has already integrated its services with automation companies like SmartThings, Insteon, Wink, etc. There are plenty of smart devices like Belkin WeMo, Sensi, Philips Hue Lights, Ecobee, and more that are compatible with Echo Dot. You can get a list of all the compatible devices from Amazon's official page for Alexa Smart Home.

With Amazon Echo Dot, you can control lights, set the temperature, or perform a wide range of tasks to make your home smarter. This is one of the best things about the device. Though, the voice command might be different from one service to another in this case. It is something that you can learn easily as and when you would use a respective service with Alexa. A few major commands can be:

- Alexa, turn the bedroom lights on (for Philips Hue lights)

- Alexa, turn the heat up to 70 (for Nest, Ecobee, etc.)

- Alexa, turn the video mode on (for Belkin WeMo)

- Alexa, turn the kitchen lights to 50% (for Philips Hue lights)

Your voice commands can change from one device to another. Additionally, with most of the devices, you might need to specify the room or area in your command. There are plenty of things you can do with Alexa smart home. The more you explore, the more amazed you would get!

Getting information

All you got to do is ask Alexa a question and she would come up with an answer instantly. Yes, it is as simple as it sounds! From the current time and weather update to a recent event – you can ask absolutely anything from Alexa.

Not only the AI can come up with an accurate answer after searching the web, but it stores information on a Cloud and keeps accessing it. Since it is based on a machine learning algorithm, it keeps learning new things. With time, the AI keeps evolving itself to serve you in a flawless way. Instead of looking on the net, you can ask Alexa questions like the following:

- Alexa, what time is it? (To get the current time of your location)

- Alexa, what time is it in London?

- Alexa, what's my commute? (To get information related to the traffic)

- Alexa, how's the weather?

- Alexa, how's the weather in Los Angeles?

Not just real-time questions, you can ask generic questions as well.

- Alexa, what is the capital of Canada?

- Alexa, how tall is the Empire State building?

- Alexa, who was the first man to climb the Mount Everest?

Alexa keeps learning new skills with time. The latest edition can use various apps as well. Though, it is not compatible with almost every app, but it can be used to deliver pizza, book a cab, order something online, and more. For instance, you can do it all by giving her commands like:

- Alexa, ask Uber to request a ride

- Alexa, ask Fitbit about my stats

- Alexa, open Domino's and ask for my Easy Order

Working as a kitchen assistant

Amazon Echo Dot can work as an amazing kitchen assistant as well. From simply searching a recipe to setting a timer, Alexa can definitely make your cooking experience a pleasant one. Are you always confused about those measurement units? Well, why not ask Alexa about it. Go ahead and try these commands:

- Alexa, tell me a recipe for chicken soup

- Alexa, how can I make an apple pie?

- Alexa, set a timer for 7 minutes

- Alexa, how many teaspoons are there in a tablespoon?

Listening to a book or a document

If you like to listen to an audiobook or simply want to read something, then Echo Dot can do it all for you. The device has been integrated with Audible (also owned by Amazon). If you have bought an audiobook from Audible, then you can simply ask Alexa to perform various tasks.

- Alexa, play audiobook *The Jungle Book* (It will start playing the book. You can swap the name of the book here.)

- Alexa, stop reading the book in 15 minutes

- Alexa, go back (go back by 30 seconds)

- Alexa, go forward (go forward by 30 seconds)

- Alexa, previous chapter

- Alexa, next chapter

- Alexa, resume my book

Also, there are plenty of Kindle Ebooks that has an inbuilt option of audio. You can access them without including the word "audiobook" in your command.

- Alexa, read *The Alchemist*

- Alexa, pause

Additionally, you can ask Alexa to extract information from a respective source and read it for you. Just follow this drill.

- Alexa, Wikipedia Australia

- Alexa, read more from Wikipedia

Alexa would simply read more from the respective source almost whatever you desire. Now, you no longer have to search for anything in the middle of the night. You can just ask Alexa to do it for you!

Being your full-time assistant

Alexa is based on IFTTT (If this then that) and therefore, it can perform a wide range of other tasks. From simply making a to-do list to setting up an alarm, the sky is the limit here. Try some of these easy commands on your own:

- Alexa, add oranges to my shopping list

- Alexa, send me my shopping list

- Alexa, set up an alarm for 6 am tomorrow

- Alexa, add jogging to my to-do list

Basic commands

Though we have included almost every major command that you can give Alexa, but there are plenty of other things you can do with Echo Dot as well. Ideally, Alexa can process almost any command. Nevertheless, here are some basic commands that you should be aware of while using your favorite device.

- Alexa, help

- Alexa, mute/unmute

- Alexa, stop/pause/resume

- Alexa, set volume to 6

- Alexa, louder

- Alexa, play (artist) station on Pandora

- Alexa, read me my Kindle book

- Alexa, add this song to my playlist

- Alexa, I like this song

- Alexa, wake me up at 6 in the morning

- Alexa, what's the day today?

- Alexa, snooze

- Alexa, what's on my calendar today?

- Alexa, create a to-do

- Alexa, add an event to my calendar

- Alexa, what's in the news?

- Alexa, will it rain today?

- Alexa, what's the traffic like?

- Alexa, find me a Chinese restaurant

- Alexa, what movies are playing?

- Alexa, find more songs by Adele

- Alexa, what is 50 times 30?

- Alexa, 8 factorial

- Alexa, how many yards are there in a mile?

- Alexa, what's the definition of (word)?

- Alexa, how do you spell (word)?

- Alexa, give me sports update

- Alexa, buy more cereals

- Alexa, track my order

- Alexa, order an Echo Dot

- Alexa, buy this song

- Alexa, discover my phone

- Alexa, give me a Harry Potter quote

- Alexa, tell me a joke

- Alexa, party time!

With Alexa, you can never really run out of commands. There are almost endless commands that you can run on Alexa. Mostly, she would be able to understand and respond promptly to it. In case if you are not happy with the result, you can always let Alexa know about it. Try to be more precise and let the AI learn from your commands to increase its vocabulary.

Finding new features

When it comes to any app or a modern device, you need to upgrade it in order to access the new features. You definitely don't have to do it all with Amazon Echo Dot. The second generation device automatically updates whenever a new upgrade is available.

Once in a while, you can always ask Alexa about the new updates with a command like –

* Alexa, what new features do you have?

The AI will let you know of any new updates and feature that it has got recently. Now, isn't that fun!

That was certainly fascinating. After a while, you would just get used to the commands and would keep inventing new ones as well. With time, Alexa would also keep improving, giving you an amazing experience.

It is definitely a fascinating device that would make your life a whole lot easier for sure! With this guide, you can definitely make the most out of it. Give your Echo Dot these commands and get to know how it would react.

Keep experimenting with your device and come up with some new commands. We are sure you are going to have a great time with your brand new Amazon Echo Dot!

Conclusion

Congratulations for finishing the guide so fast! We are sure you must have had a great time learning all these amazing things about the new Echo Dot device from this guide. The second generation Echo Dot is one of the best devices that has been produced by Amazon and has so many things to offer.

In this comprehensive guide, we tried to make you familiar with almost everything that this AI-enabled device can do. Firstly, we made you set up your device using a list of easy instructions. Also, to help you use other devices with your Echo Dot, we provided an in-depth walkthrough. By following our simple instructions, you can connect your Echo Dot with other devices easily.

After covering all the major specifications, we made you familiar with almost everything that Alexa can do. To make things simpler for you, we have provided an application-based usage of the device. After going through this guide, you can easily learn how to use Alexa as a kitchen-assistance or an audiobook reader.

There are certainly thousands of things that you can do with Alexa and we tried to cover the basics of everything in our guide. We also came up with a list of all the essential commands that you should be familiar with. You can easily turn your house smarter or work on a science project with Alexa by your side.

We tried to come up with a quick and informative guide to making you an expert user of Amazon Echo Dot. Now when you are well-informed, you can definitely make the most out of your favorite device.

Use your Amazon Echo Dot wisely. We are sure that the second generation Echo Dot will definitely be an integral part of your life in no time.

FREE Bonus Reminder

If you have not grabbed it yet, please go ahead and download your special bonus report *"DIY Projects. 13 Useful & Easy To Make DIY Projects To Save Money & Improve Your Home!"*

Simply Click the Button Below

OR **Go to This Page**

http://diyhomecraft.com/free

BONUS #2: More Free & Discounted Books or Products

Do you want to receive more Free/Discounted Books or Products?

We have a mailing list where we send out our new Books or Products when they go free or with a discount on Amazon. Click on the link below to sign up for Free & Discount Book & Product Promotions.

=> Sign Up for Free & Discount Book & Product Promotions <=

OR Go to this URL

http://zbit.ly/1WBb1Ek